Booker T. Washington

written by **Joeming Dunn**
illustrated by **Chris Allen**

magic wagon

visit us at
www.abdopublishing.com

Published by Magic Wagon, a division of the ABDO Publishing Group, 8000 West 78th Street, Edina, Minnesota 55439.

Printed in the United States.

Written by Joeming Dunn
Illustrated by Chris Allen
Edited by Stephanie Hedlund and Rochelle Baltzer
Interior layout and design by Antarctic Press
Cover art by Chris Allen and Rod Espinosa
Cover design by Neil Klinepier

Library of Congress Cataloging-in-Publication Data

Dunn, Joeming W.
Booker T. Washington / written by Joeming Dunn ; illustrated by Chris Allen.
p. cm. -- (Bio-graphics)
Includes index.
ISBN 978-1-60270-177-9
1. Washington, Booker T., 1856-1915--Juvenile literature. 2. African Americans--Biography--Juvenile literature. 3. Educators--United States--Biography--Juvenile literature. I. Allen, Chris, 1972- ill. II. Title.

E185.97.W4D86 2009
370.92--dc22
[B] 2007051500

TABLE of CONTENTS

Timeline

1856 - Booker T. Washington was born a slave on April 5.

1865 - The Civil War ended and Washington became one of the 4 million slaves to be freed.

1872 - Washington left his home to attend the Hampton Agricultural Institute.

1875 - Washington graduated from the Hampton Agricultural Institute with honors.

1881 - At age 25, Washington opened the Tuskegee Normal and Industrial Institute on July 4.

1895 - Washington delivered *The Atlanta Address* at the Cotton States and International Exposition.

1896 - Washington was presented with an honorary degree from Harvard University.

1900 - Washington founded the National Negro Business League.

1915 - Washington died at home in Tuskegee, Alabama, on November 14.

Chapter 1 Born a Slave
Booker T. Washington was born on April 5, 1856, on a farm in Hale's Ford, Virginia. He was born into slavery.
WHAT A BEAUTIFUL BABY. I'LL NAME YA BOOKER.
His mother was a cook.
His father was a white man who worked on another farm. No one knew his name.

His mother later married a slave named Washington Ferguson. That is when Booker took the name Washington.
I DO!
I PRONOUNCE YOU HUSBAND AND WIFE.
Soon afterward, the Civil War ended. Slavery ended in the United States.
Booker was now free, at the age of nine. He and his family moved to Malden, West Virginia.
WE CAN MOVE WHEREVER WE WANT.

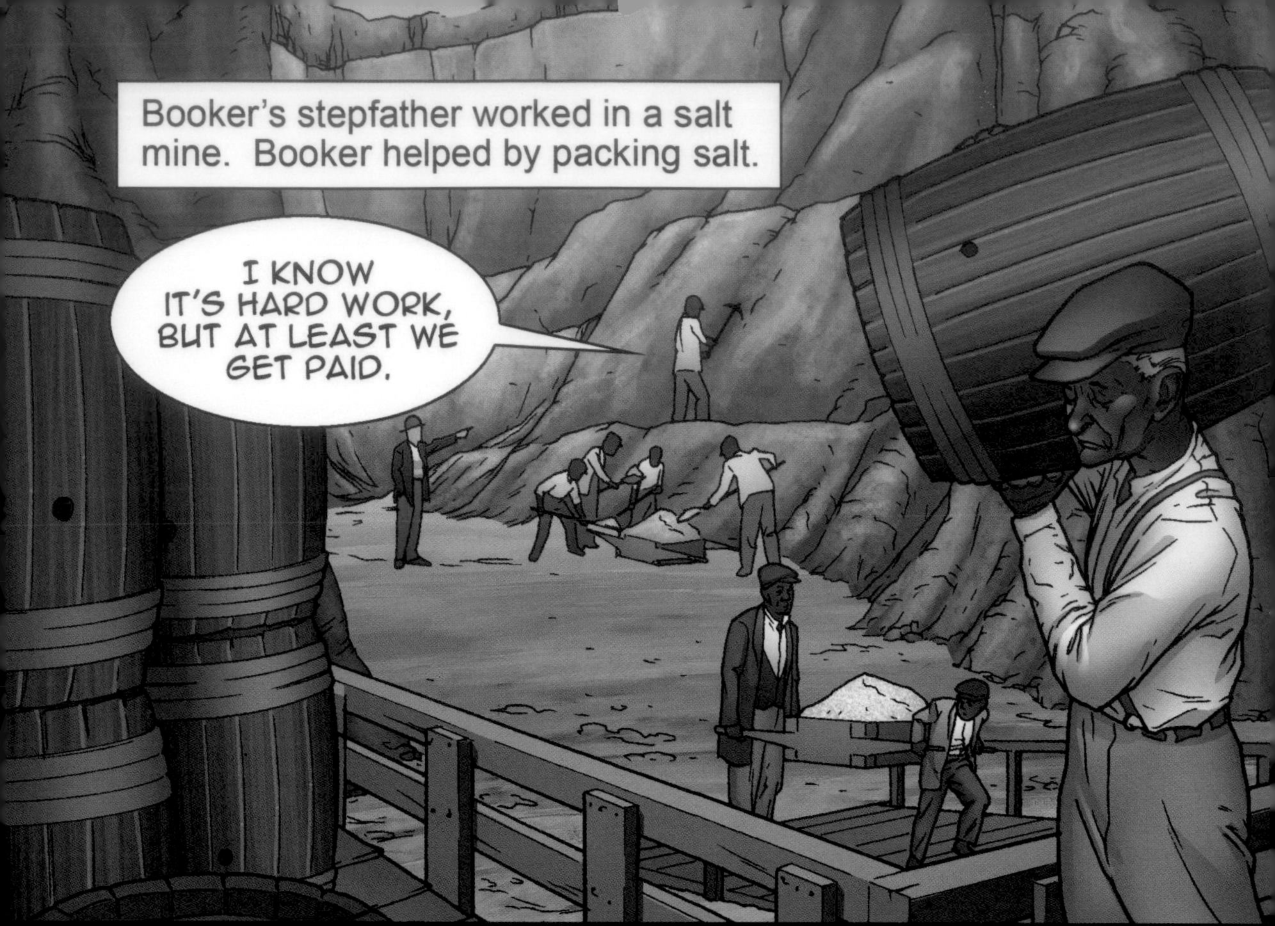
Booker's stepfather worked in a salt mine. Booker helped by packing salt.
I KNOW IT'S HARD WORK, BUT AT LEAST WE GET PAID.

As he grew older, Booker also worked on a steamboat.

Booker soon became the house servant of Viola Ruffner. Her husband, General Lewis Ruffner, owned the salt and coal mines.

Mrs. Ruffner was very stern and demanding.
WHAT KIND OF WORK IS THIS?
THIS IS TERRIBLE! WHAT A LOUSY JOB.

Chapter 2 Early Education

Booker worked very hard to meet Mrs. Ruffner's high standards. She noticed his efforts.
She saw potential in Booker and encouraged him to learn to read and write.
WHY DON'T YOU READ THIS BOOK?
THANK YOU, MA'AM.
He soon learned to read and write. He longed to learn more.

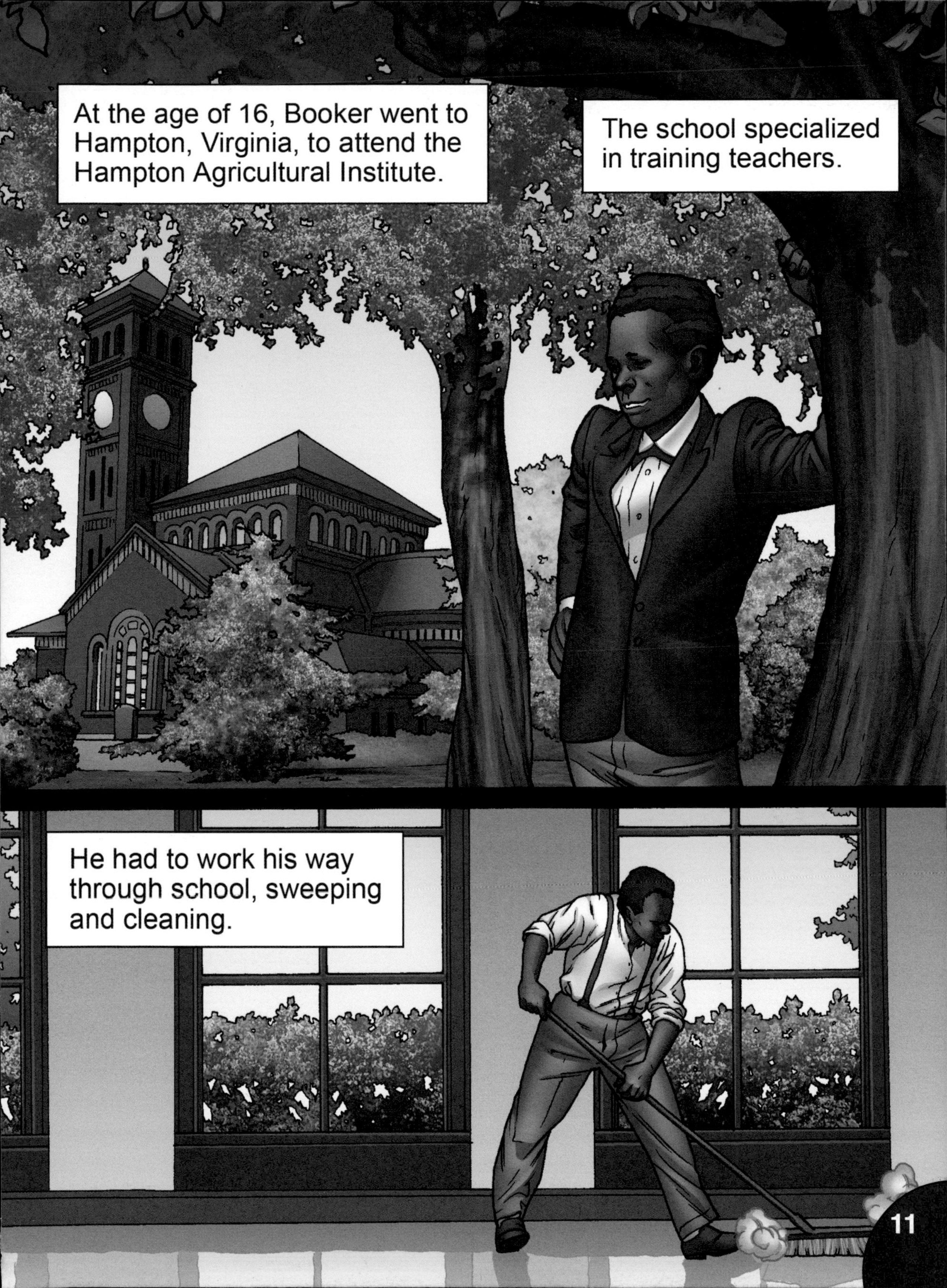
At the age of 16, Booker went to Hampton, Virginia, to attend the Hampton Agricultural Institute.
The school specialized in training teachers.
He had to work his way through school, sweeping and cleaning.

Booker graduated from Hampton Institute in 1875.

Afterward, he taught for a few years. He later attended Wayland Seminary in Washington, D.C., for a year.

In 1880, a former slave named Lewis Adams worked to advance African Americans.
YOU SHOULD VOTE FOR THESE MEN.
THEY WILL HELP EDUCATE YOU.
He helped two candidates win a local election in Macon County, Alabama.

When both men were elected, they helped get money to build the Tuskegee Normal and Industrial Institute. This school was specifically for African Americans.
IT MAY NOT BE MUCH, BUT IT'S A START.

Chapter 3 Principal Washington

A principal was needed for the new school. Adams talked to Samuel Armstrong about finding the right person.
BUT I HAVE A PERSON THAT IS PERFECT FOR THE JOB.
Armstrong was principal at Hampton, where Washington worked.
Washington was given the job. The school opened on July 4, 1881. It was known for teaching practical education.
Subjects included farming, carpentry, and bricklaying.
WE WILL GIVE YOUNG PEOPLE THE SKILLS THEY NEED TO BECOME GOOD CITIZENS.

Soon, the school moved to an abandoned plantation. The students built many of the new buildings.
Washington believed that African Americans needed to be self-reliant. He also felt they should show loyalty to the United States and prove they had rights.
DON'T EXPECT EVERYTHING JUST BECAUSE WE ARE NOW FREE.
In 1882, Washington married Fanny Norton Smith. They had a child together. Sadly, Fanny died two years later.

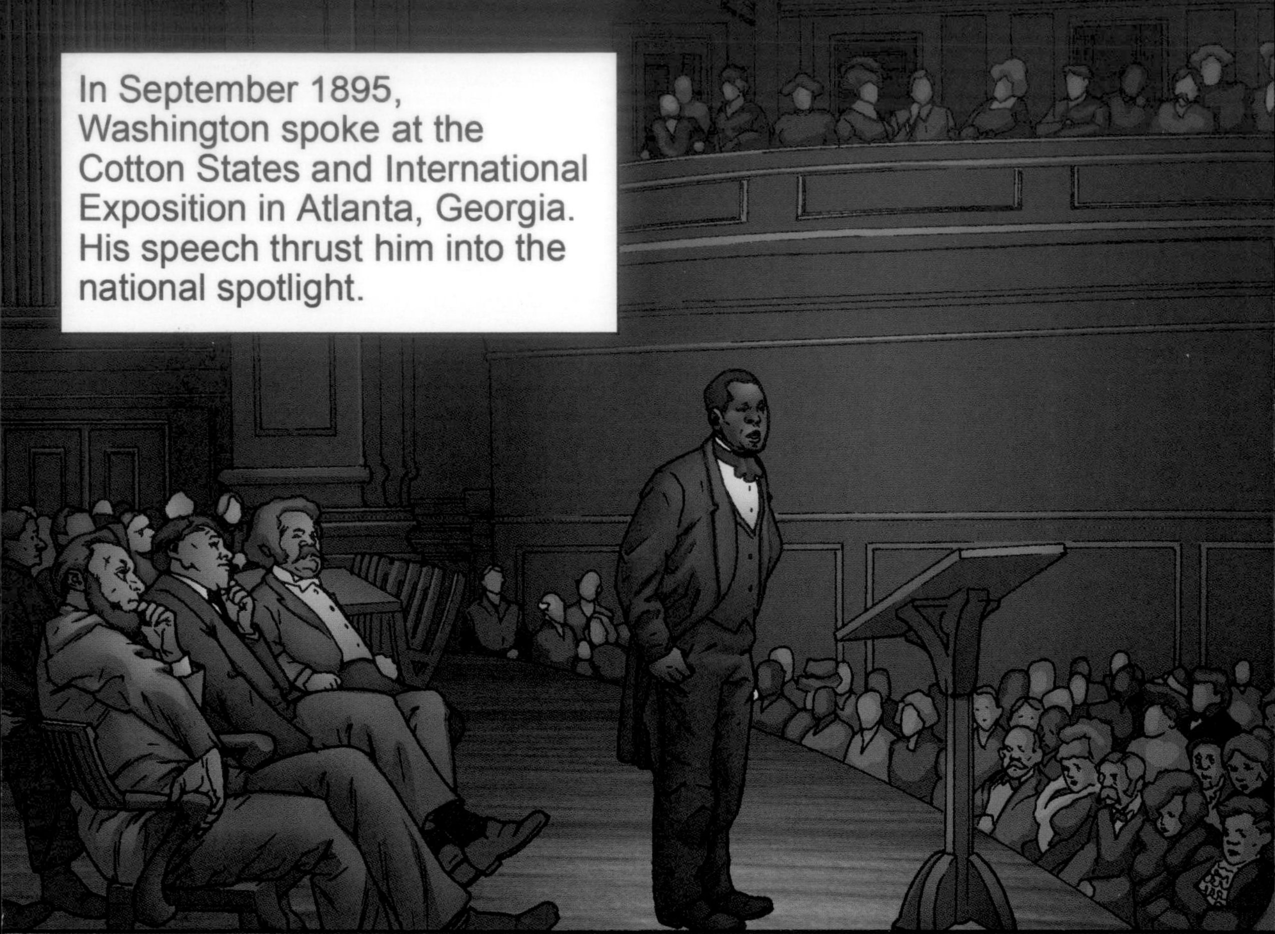
In September 1895, Washington spoke at the Cotton States and International Exposition in Atlanta, Georgia. His speech thrust him into the national spotlight.

Many prominent African Americans at the time wanted greater action for the community. Some, like Frederick Douglass, wanted to agitate for changes. Others, like W.E.B. Du Bois, thought education was best used for the top 10 percent.

Washington had a different approach. He wanted to find a middle ground between the white and African-American communities.
WE HAVE TO BECOME SELF-RELIANT AND IMPROVE OURSELVES.
WE HAVE TO ACCEPT SEGREGATION AS A MEANS TO AN END.

Du Bois and many others did not like Washington's opinion. They felt he was trying to please the white people.
BOOKER SHOULD BE CALLED "THE GREAT ACCOMMODATOR."

While Washington had critics, he also had supporters. They included his daughter and his new wife, Olivia America Davidson, and their two sons.

Chapter 4 A New Cause

Washington's viewpoints also made him popular with many politicians, including President William McKinley. McKinley even visited the Tuskegee Institute. Unfortunately, the president was assassinated soon afterward.
I WANT TO THANK YOU FOR YOUR WORK.
I AM HONORED WITH YOUR VISIT.

Washington then visited the White House. He met with President Theodore Roosevelt soon after Roosevelt took office. Washington was the first African-American invited to the White House.

Many wealthy philanthropists, including Andrew Carnegie and Henry Rogers, supported Washington's ideas and opinions. They donated money to help him further his cause of education.

Washington spoke to many people. He promoted his idea of improving both economic and social relations between African Americans and whites.
WE MUST WORK TOGETHER.

Many African-Americans still criticized Washington. They said he was not really looking after their best interests but trying to get money.
WASHINGTON, D.C.
12
C 82
12
1889

In 1900, Washington established and served as president of the National Negro Business League.
IT IS IMPORTANT FOR US TO ESTABLISH OURSELVES IN THE COMMUNITY.

The purpose of the organization was to help African Americans start a new business or acquire property.
DEED

Chapter 5 Fighting Segregation

In 1901, an autobiography of Booker's life called *Up From Slavery* was published. It influenced many Americans.
Up From Slavery
by
BOOKER T. WASHINGTON

The book spread Washington's goal of self-help and empowerment. It inspired future African-American leaders, including Marcus Garvey, Elijah Muhammad, and Malcolm X.

Many people did not agree with Washington. They felt that Washington did not do enough for African Americans. Du Bois and others spoke against him.
MR. WASHINGTON NEEDS NOT TO PLEASE THOSE THAT HAVE GIVEN HIM MONEY.
Some felt that Washington did not address many of the inequalities that existed. At that time, voting and civil rights were not equal for African Americans.
BALLOT
EQUAL RIGHTS FOR ALL
EQUAL RIGHTS FOR ALL
ALL MEN ARE CREATED

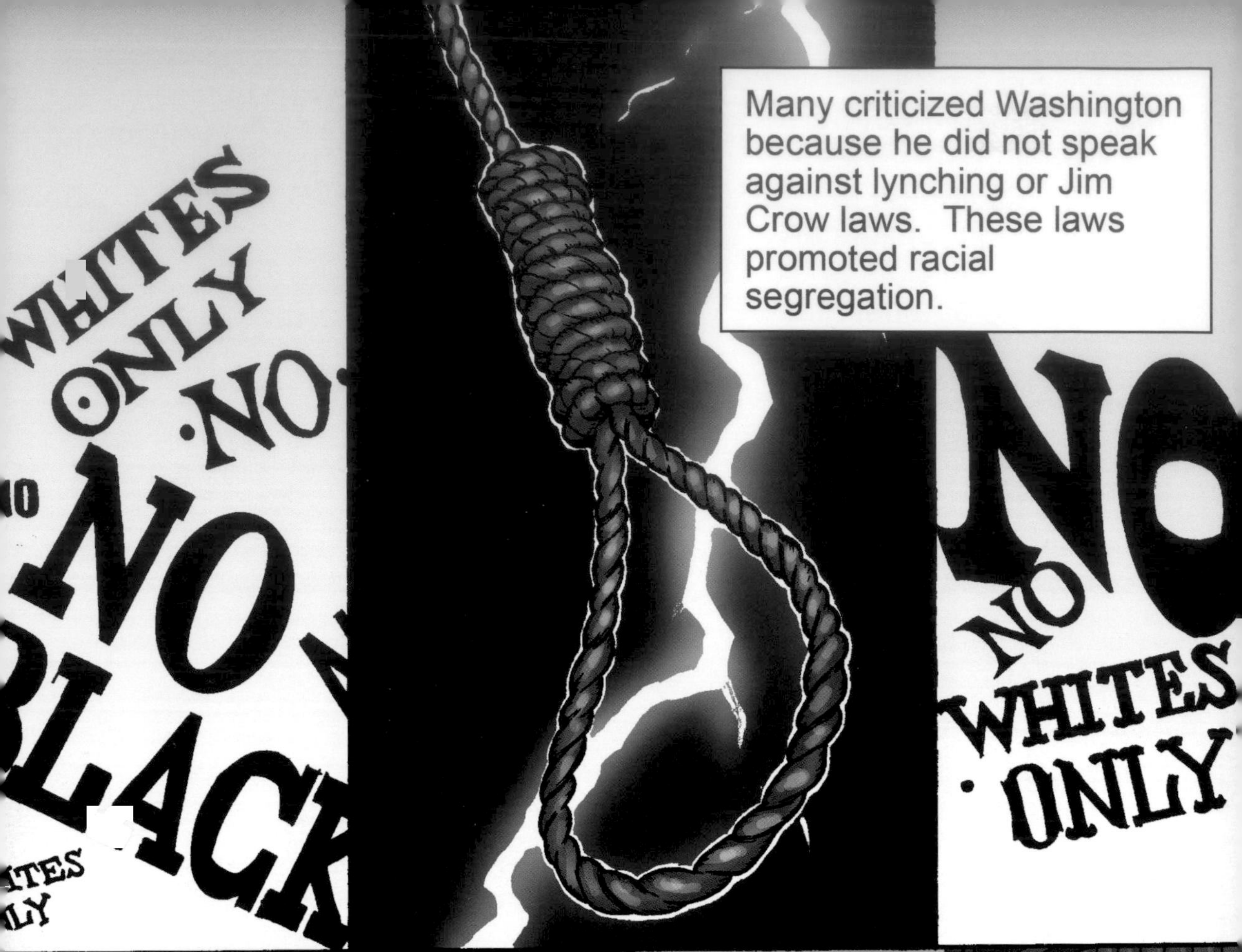
Many criticized Washington because he did not speak against lynching or Jim Crow laws. These laws promoted racial segregation.
WHITES ONLY
NO
NO
WHITES ONLY
NO

These critics did not know that Washington contributed his knowledge and money to help fight segregation.

Chapter 6 Many Honors

Due to his many works, Washington received honorary degrees from both Harvard University and Dartmouth College.
THANK YOU FOR THIS HONOR.
Washington became the spokesperson for the education of African Americans. Many schools and homes for African Americans were built due to his efforts.
SMITH'S TAILORING

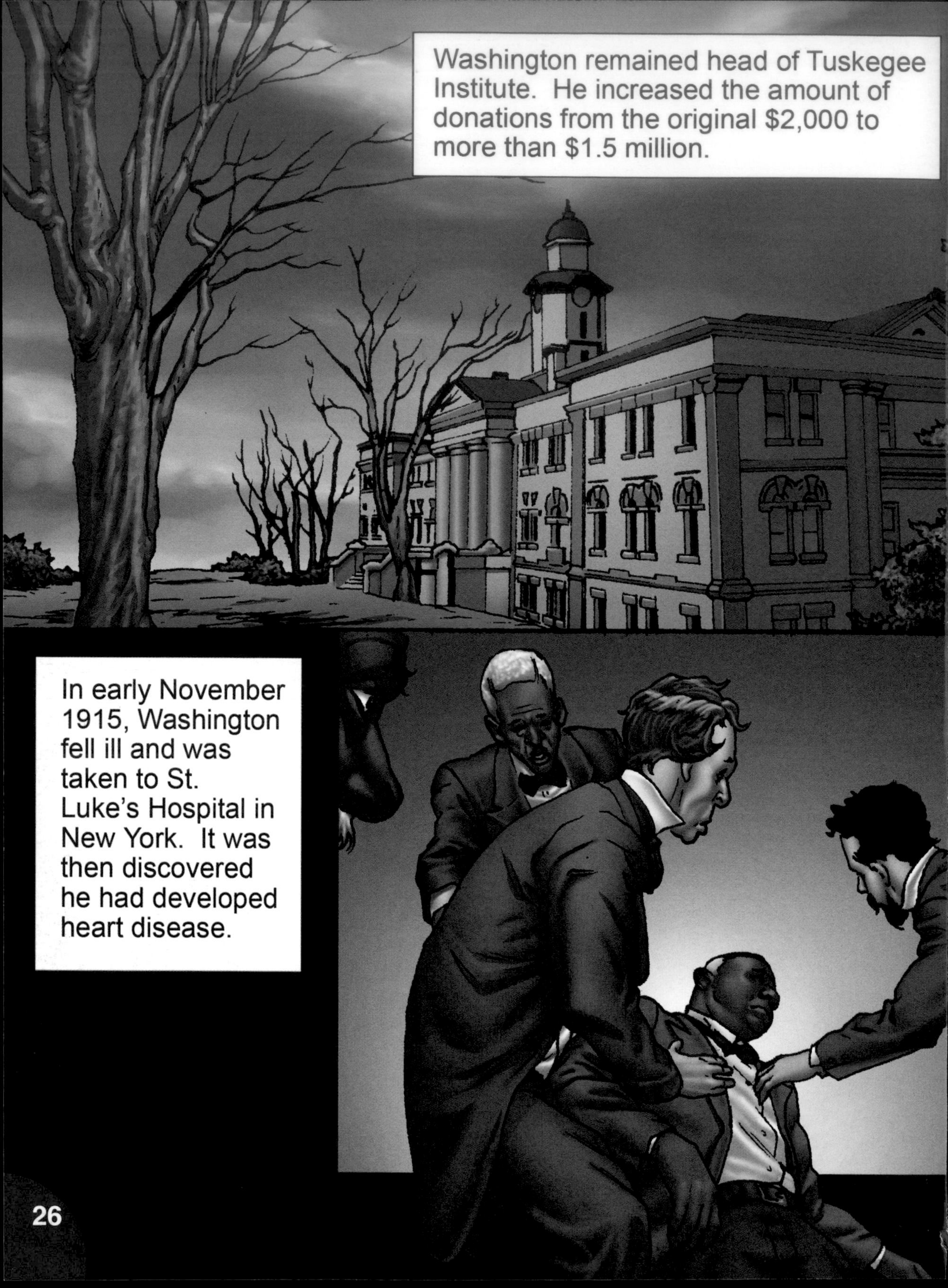
Washington remained head of Tuskegee Institute. He increased the amount of donations from the original $2,000 to more than $1.5 million.
In early November 1915, Washington fell ill and was taken to St. Luke's Hospital in New York. It was then discovered he had developed heart disease.

Washington returned to Tuskegee, Alabama, where he died on November 14, 1915.
More than 8,000 people attended his funeral.

Washington was honored in many ways. He was the first African American to be featured on a stamp and a U.S. coin.

His house in Virginia was turned into a national monument. Each year, thousands of people visit the Booker T. Washington National Monument to learn about his life.

Many may have disagreed with the ideas and opinions of Booker T. Washington. Yet, his life and influence will leave an impression for years to come.

Further Reading

Amper, Thomas. *Booker T. Washington*. Minneapolis: Lerner Publishing Group, 2003.

Gosda, Randy T. *Booker T. Washington*. First Biography. Edina: ABDO Publishing Company, 2002.

McKissack, Patricia and Fredrick. *Booker T. Washington: Leader and Educator*. Berkeley Heights: Enslow Publishing, 2001.

Nicholson, Lois P. *Booker T. Washington - Educator/Activist: A Modern Moses*. New York: Facts on File, 1998.

Glossary

agitate - to stir up discussion.

assassinate - to murder a very important person, usually for political reasons.

criticize - to find fault with something. People who voice their opinions are called critics.

lynch - to put to death without trial, usually performed by a mob of people.

philanthropist - someone who actively promotes the welfare of all human beings by speaking for rights and providing money.

potential - capable of being or becoming. Something that is possible, but not actual.

prominent - widely known.

segregation - the separation of an individual or a group from a larger group.

self-reliant - using one's own efforts to provide food, clothing, and other necessities.

spokesperson - a person who is a representative of a product in order to encourage others to purchase that item. Often a spokesperson is a celebrity or a recognizable public figure.

Web Sites

To learn more about Booker T. Washington, visit ABDO Publishing Company on the World Wide Web at www.abdopublishing.com. Web sites about Washington are featured on our Book Links page. These links are routinely monitored and updated to provide the most current information available.

Index